T0198993

MICHAEL CAHILL

FROM
Pearl Harbor
TO
9/11

One Final Mission for Love of the United States
to Respect, Heal, and Remember

AuthorHouse™
1663 Liberty Drive
Bloomington, IN 47403
www.authorhouse.com
Phone: 1 (800) 839-8640

© *2019 Michael Cahill. All rights reserved.*

No part of this book may be reproduced, stored in a retrieval system,
or transmitted by any means without the written permission of the author.

Published by AuthorHouse 01/18/2019

ISBN: 978-1-5462-7101-7 (sc)
ISBN: 978-1-5462-7103-1 (hc)
ISBN: 978-1-5462-7102-4 (e)

Library of Congress Control Number: 2018914393

Print information available on the last page.

Any people depicted in stock imagery provided by Getty Images are models,
and such images are being used for illustrative purposes only.
Certain stock imagery © Getty Images.

This book is printed on acid-free paper.

Because of the dynamic nature of the Internet, any web addresses or links contained in this book may have changed
since publication and may no longer be valid. The views expressed in this work are solely those of the author and do not
necessarily reflect the views of the publisher, and the publisher hereby disclaims any responsibility for them.

authorHOUSE®

FROM PEARL HARBOR TO 9/11

ONE FINAL MISSION FOR LOVE OF THE UNITED STATES TO RESPECT, HEAL, AND REMEMBER

Michael Cahill

Thanks to all those that made this possible:

Diane Pirzada, Executive historical consultant

Emily Kopke Artistic director

Heidi Hayden, Former Chief People Officer, 9/11 Memorial

Lt. Col. Richard Vargus United States Pentagon

Captain John Kerwick

Nicola Wales-Wong

Linda Blick, Co Chair, Tails of Hope Foundation copywrite 2017

Robert Reeg, FDNY Survivor 9/11

Police Chief Timothy Griffen

Bill Buck Chevrolet

The United States Army 25th Infantry Tropical Lightning

The Greatest Generations Foundation

Denis V. Cooper Foundation

KP Pezeshkan, Manhattan Building Company, Naples Florida

The 9/11 Memorial

Fire Department New York City

New York City Police Department

American Airlines

Sarasota Sheriffs Department

Florida State Highway Patrol

Tails of Hope Foundation copywrite 2017

Tom Rudd Photography copywrite 2017

Lisa Pflaum Photography copywrite 2017

Mary Kulakowski Photograph copywrite 2017

Jessica Sanchez Wink News

US Intrepid staff

Vietnam Veteran Motorcycle club

All those that donated through the years.

Michael Cahill, Author

THE COST OF FREEDOM IS NOT FREE. THANK YOU TO ALL OUR VETERANS FOR YOUR SERVICE.

"I have been to hell"
From Pearl Harbor to 9/11

I have been to hell

Walking out the doors of hanger one

everything seemed settled

My head turned hearing a hum in the sky

It was not the red circles I wanted to see

as they flew closer and louder

hell broke loose

bullets raining on all sides of me

planes flying so low I watched pilots laughing

shot back four clips of ammo

bombs exploding everywhere

in 15 minutes it was destroyed

I was alive

There is hatred, anger in my soul

to live another day on Guadalcanal

or not.

Brutal, barbaric, fight or die

We fought, I lived- barley

stabbed in the calf, knocked down by malaria

saved by a Marine corps brother and Red Cross Angel

lucky, very grateful to go home

years later a letter from an enemy solder

both doing what we were asked by our country

He asked for understanding

to heal the wounds

At last inner peace after 50 years

time to spread my passion

Time has me growing older tougher

I asked my friends to get me to NYC

A deep need to pay my respects to those lost

My chance is granted

One final mission to respect, heal and remember

performing one final anthem

Now almost 95

Still refuse to sit

Helped to my feet

I stand and salute all those lost

I salute our flag, and this country I love

To remember those that served before, now and after me

please remember the whole war

never be anxious to start another

I am at peace, its heaven

My name is Michael Cahill. I had the honor and privilege to know, care for, and call Pearl Harbor survivor John Seelie my friend during the last four years of his life. John had one of the sharpest minds, quickest wits, and greatest love for this country I have ever known. John Seelie was a treasured national hero to me, to those he met, and to those who knew him. John was one of the toughest people I ever knew. I never found anyone in the four years I knew him who did not admire and appreciate him.

John Seelie was stationed that morning at Hanger 1, Schofield Barracks, Wheeler Airfield. He was one of the first to hear and see the Japanese planes attack. Seventy-six years and six months after the attack on Pearl Harbor, he was driven by his love for America to honor, remember, and pay his respects to those lost on September 11, forever tying together the two attacks on American soil. This is his story in many of his own words.

"My name is John Seelie. I was at Schofield Barracks and Wheeler Field on December 7, 1941. I was a corporal in the army in the Twenty-Fifth Division. I was assigned to Wheeler Field for guard duty that morning. The airplanes were lined up in three rows. When the Japanese came in, all they had to do was come straight down the line, strafe them, and bomb them. When I first saw the planes come in, I thought they were all American planes coming in until they got close enough for us to see the wings. I was only about ten feet from the front of the hangar. When the first plane came over, the first shell went through the hangar wall about a foot from my head. I think I fired four clips of ammunition. It was probably not the best way to try to knock down a plane.

"They wiped out the field in fifteen minutes. The whole field had fifteen to twenty bomb holes in it. The planes were all destroyed. The hangars were mostly destroyed. We jumped into two-and-a-half-ton trucks and headed down the beach and up to the mountains. We were very angry because the shock had worn off by that time. We were up there for about a week before they brought us down. From that point on, we were in intensive jungle training. Nobody had any idea where we were going, but we all knew we were going someplace. I hope that people remember Pearl Harbor. They will remember the whole war and not be so anxious to start another one."[1]

After contracting malaria, he was transferred to a hospital in New Zealand.

I met John Seelie while watching Cleveland Browns football games late in the season at a tavern in Englewood in 2013. We were both from Cleveland. There is something about living in a city like Cleveland where nothing is given, nothing is easy, and everything is earned. He was dressed in Browns gear and a US Army ball cap—nothing that would indicate any part of his background. He was quiet and had his Heineken resting in a cup of ice so it would not warm as he took his time sipping it. We struck up typical small talk. I would not see or talk to him again until the beginning of the 2014 football season.

---

[1] Vimeo video produced by ESPN. Amy Stokes NFL

After a game on November 30, 2014, it was raining hard as the game ended. Everyone was waiting out the downpour, and we got to talking. He mentioned that he had watched Babe Ruth play ball by sneaking under the gate at League Park as a very young kid. When I found out John was a big baseball fan, I asked, "How old are you?"

He responded, "I am ninety-two." He mentioned he had to get going. He still drove, and he explained that he needed to find a ride to the airport at five o'clock in the morning on Tuesday, December 2, 2014. He said he had to make some calls.

I asked why he needed get to the airport by five o'clock.

He told me they were sending him back.

I asked, "Back to where?"

He responded, "Honolulu."

I asked, "Why would someone be sending you back to Honolulu at the age of ninety-two? And why would you have to be at the airport at five o'clock in the morning?"

He said, "They are sending me back to Pearl Harbor."

I asked, "Are you a Pearl Harbor survivor?"

He responded, "Yes."

The Greatest Generation Foundation was picking up his entire week's tab in Hawaii to remember the seventy-third anniversary of Pearl Harbor. All he had to do was get to the airport and back.

I took down his phone number, address, and the numbers of his contact people. I had one day to work on his ride. It just hit me the wrong way that any veteran—let alone a Pearl Harbor survivor— would be looking for a ride, especially for one as important and simple as a ride to the airport. The next day was December 1. I had one workday to get something—anything—done for him.

I called a limousine company and told them about John and his need for a ride to the airport.

They said, "Yes—no charge."

I reached out to a news crew and asked if they had any interest in covering him leaving for his return to Hawaii. I got another yes. I thought, *What else? An honor guard to send him off would be nice.* Within half an hour, three men returned my call and said they would be in his driveway in the early hours to send him off.

I decided to push a little further, and I contacted the sheriff's department and the state highway patrol. I asked for a lights-on escort of the limousine from his home to the airport. I explained the circumstance.

They nicely explained that without a formal application, which had to be supplied months before, and approval, they were not able to do anything. They took my contact information.

At one o'clock that afternoon, I got a call from the sheriff. They were making a special exception and were going to escort John's limousine to the airport. At four fifteen, I got another call from the state highway patrol. They were going to make an exception and escort his limousine to the airport.

I arranged for the limousine, news coverage, an honor guard, and a police send-off. I knew it was going to shock him. The respect for these special survivors shocked me.

That next morning, in the dark, I watched it all unfold. I stood in front of his home as the limo pulled in. The news crew started broadcasting from outside his home and then moved inside. John was wearing his Pearl Harbor survivor's cover, a Hawaiian shirt, and white dress pants.

When John brought out his huge *Titanic*-era suitcase, three honor guards, a sheriff, and a state trooper—in dress uniforms—all snapped to attention and saluted. This caught us both off guard, and John got a little emotional.

I watched it all with a few friends and neighbors who knew he was making the trip back to Hawaii. Some held small American flags and watched in the dark from across the street. He never knew I was there.

As the patrol car turned on its lights, John entered the limousine. The officers helped with his bag and walker, and off they went. The sheriff from Sarasota County drove to the county line, and a sheriff's patrol car from Lee County seamlessly filled in behind the limousine.

Upon arrival, John was greeted by as many applauding TSA agents and airport personnel as could be there. John spent seven days at Pearl Harbor and had a wonderful time.

I picked up John at the airport when he got back, and we kept in touch.

John was really tired and was not getting much of his energy back.

By January, he was having trouble breathing.

I asked if he wanted to get it checked.

He drove himself to the hospital and was diagnosed with pneumonia in both lungs. When I got to the hospital, I found out he had also had many bouts of malaria over the years. They gave him antibiotics, and three days later, like a miracle, his lungs were clear. He went home and started going to the gym again.

John was a gym rat. Every day, he parked diagonally in the striped fire zone by the door. Nobody said a thing. He went to the gym five or six days a week for three hours at a time. For the final fifty minutes or so, he would swim without touching the bottom. He believed that he had to stay fit to travel back to Pearl Harbor. He wanted to make it to the seventy-fifth remembrance.

We kept in touch after that, going to grab bites from time to time. I made sure he had what he needed, often stopping to pick up food or batteries for his hearing aids. He would give me a twenty-dollar bill, and I would give him his change. When I would hand him his change, it would always be for the entire amount he gave me, just broken into smaller bills. I smiled, wondering how long I could get away with this tactic.

He started to feel comfortable around me and began to open up a little. He spoke about his wife of sixty-two-and-a-half years who had passed, his family, business dealings, and then his service. He would call me and ask if I had time for this or that or a bite.

Whenever he called, he would say, "Hi, Mike. It's Seelie." He never used his first name. Whenever he called or asked about something, I made a decision to be there for the guy.

One rule was no talking or calling during Cleveland Indians games. Whenever I would call him, he had the TV blaring loudly and would never pick up. I always had to call multiple times.

We watched terrible Cleveland Browns football and shared pizzas and other bites. John started opening up about the war to me in early 2015. After a short time, I knew if he wanted to get breakfast, he needed to talk about the war. Lunch was half of it. He just wanted to get out of the house, or he talked about growing up or the war.

Dinner was always for fun and lots of dumb jokes. Dinner was at a beach restaurant called Lock and Key restaurant in Englewood Florida.

John was a girl magnet. Women would give him hugs and kisses on his cheeks and forehead. At one point, he looked at me and said, "I am doing okay, kid. You need to step up your game."

I thought, *Step up my game?*

I began to call his phrases "Johnisms." At breakfast, he would always order waffles with a lot of butter and coffee, and then he would talk. I asked if he felt better after telling me things that had been inside him for more than seventy years. I think it helped him, and I know it helped me

John lost his funding back to Pearl Harbor 74 on November 9, 2015. The reason given is that they could not find enough Pearl Harbor survivors to meet funding requirements. They needed six and had three. I found out this was not true in 2017. Survivors normally traveled on December 2 or 3. I did not have a lot of time. I asked if he really needed to go that year.

He said, "That's what I live for. It's the only place I can go where they remember what happened and who I am, and I am grateful. I am going—even if I have to swim there."

I got an emotional lump in my throat.

I went to work for him. I asked for and received first-class tickets in both directions from American Airlines. It took one call and a couple of emails. Thank you, American Airlines!

I asked John if he would help me by providing some interviews for papers and television.

He was all in.

I gambled when I set up an interview to highlight him losing his funding with a television station I knew was syndicated. I hoped that other stations around the country would pick up on his story.

When we saw the attractive reporter in the parking lot, I made a comment to John that she was so young we might have to walk her through the interview.

Jessica Sanchez from Wink News stepped up to the plate with her first set of questions and knocked the interview out of the park. She used a new-school technique for an old-school subject. We did an incredibly detailed television interview with her in hopes of—after a nice edit—getting donations for his travel on our GoFundMe account.

After it aired, hundreds of donations adding up to thousands of dollars poured in.

I got a call from K. P. Pezeshkan, vice president of Manhattan Building Company in Naples, and they funded everything else without condition. The total value of funding raised in nine days was more than $11,400.

By November 20, 2015, John was fully funded and booked at the Hyatt Waikiki Beach in Honolulu. I decided that it would not serve John well for me to get him there and not know the territory. He knew Honolulu like his hometown. I knew nothing.

I asked James Owen, curator of the Pearl Harbor Museum, and Jessi Higa, a Pearl Harbor event coordinator, to find me a knowledgeable local concierge. They provided me with three names, indicating that while all were top-notch, Nicola Wales-Wong was really recommended—if she was available.

I was sending my friend halfway around the world by himself. I needed to know he was going to be treated as well as possible. I asked for references from all three candidates and grilled everyone—from half a world away.

Nicola seemed to be heads above the others. I called her, and we talked, and then I asked her to send a picture of herself and a picture of her driver's license. I was pleasantly surprised, and I hired her. Her effort and professionalism were remarkable!

John spent ten days in Honolulu and had a great time.

John called me on Nicola's phone and asked if I could run "interference" from his family for him. He told me that he and Nicola had gotten married ten minutes ago. Before he hung up, I could hear them both having a good laugh at my expense!

Nicola spent extra time making certain he was okay after he fell ill from eating an egg salad sandwich. Nicola took him to the NFL Pro Bowl, which started at 6:00 a.m. in Hawaii and got him to all the activities, parades, and dinners he wanted.

Years later, I am still honored to call her my friend. We talk often, but we have never met in person. The Greatest Generation Foundation noticed her professional efforts in caring for John and was so impressed that they hired her.

John and I kept in touch throughout 2016. On Sundays, we would go out to lunch or dinner. I also set him up with video interviews and print interviews.

Since he was funded to return to the seventy-fifth anniversary by the Greatest Generation Foundation, I decided to provide John with a custom-embroidered Hawaiian shirt. The shirt would tell the story of his service, his family, and his life. I placed an ad on Craigslist: "I need an artist who can draw with a pencil—not just a computer."

The ad specifically said the project was for a Pearl Harbor survivor, and I had more than fifty responses. After several interviews in June, I met an incredibly talented young artist. She was so impressive with her sketching skills, and she wanted to do it. She provided me with pencil sketches of bugs, vertebra, and some graphics. I gave her the job.

Emily Kopke liked to be called simply Emi, and she was a freshman at the University of Miami. We worked through the summer on the various items that needed to be represented on the shirt. Emi did her homework, making certain all the artwork was as correct and historically accurate as possible. The first time she saw it, the smile on her face said it all. The shirt took everyone's breath away! Even as the machine sewed thousands of stitches, the embroidery shop took on a feeling that something big was happening.

December 7, 2016

SCHOFIELD BARRACKS
WHEELER ARMY AIRFIELD

Pearl Harbor
December 7, 1941

E PLURIBUS UNUM

75

December 7, 2016

SCHOFIELD BARRACKS
WHEELER ARMY AIRFIELD

Guadalcanal
New Georgia Island

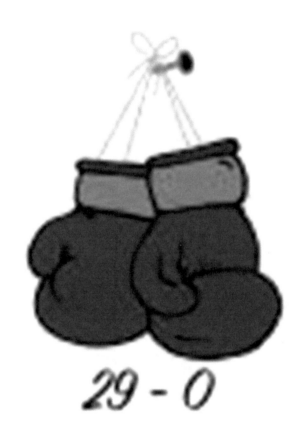

29 - 0

U.S. ARMY | JOHN SEELIE

December 7, 2016

December 7, 1941
Remember Pearl Harbor

25th Infantry

Tropical Lightning

With all my
love
Betty

There was special celebration honoring John on Veterans Day 2016 at Lemon Bay High School. John's daughter Denise was in town and looked thrilled that she could partake in these activities with her dad. Emi met John and gave him his shirt in a packed gym with an emotional standing ovation from 1,200 students and staff. The staff and some of the students teared up. Many were taken in by the reality of having history stand in front of them. Most students had only read about Pearl Harbor in history books as if it were a footnote. The line to meet him was impressive.

Later that day, John was honored in a wall of chalk art that depicted him looking back in time seventy-five years at a burning Pearl Harbor at the 2016 Venice Chalk Festival. John had a police escort to the festival grounds. The motorcade consisted of two police cars, a polished black SUV, complete with US Army decals and American flags above the doors, donated for the event by Bill Buck Chevrolet, a World War II Jeep and a World War II troop carrier.

The event was broadcast live on Facebook at 1:48 p.m. in Florida, which was the exact time of morning in Honolulu when the attack began. People from all over the world were watching. A couple hundred people, including the mayor, gathered to see John exit his ride and stand next to a chalk picture of the burning *Arizona* in Pearl Harbor. He was greeted by a four-member color guard that stood at attention the entire time. The event ended with John in the middle of the color guard and the commander calling the salute.

John went back to Pearl Harbor for the last time seventy-five years later. He was ninety-four. He was flying out of Tampa, and I hired a driver to take us. We arrive about three hours early. There were four news crews waiting for him.

I took the flag from in front of his home and draped it across his wheelchair. John could still walk; the chair saved his energy. A large crowd gathered around him, hugging and kissing him and shaking his hand.

I noticed pilots and crew leaving their planes and coming over to shake his hand and take pictures with him. When an announcement was made over the airport speakers, the applause began. It never really let up.

The reporters lined up to get a few words from this American veteran. John had a wonderful week in Honolulu. His daughter spent the week there to experience it with her father. He knew it was his last trip there, and he made the most of remembering, smiling, exchanging stories, and taking it all in.

I asked him to go to Schofield Barracks and stand in the exact spot he was on December 7, 1941. The pictures show the spray of bullets around him and over his head.

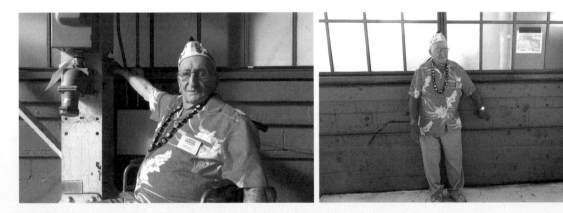

John was very tired when he came back from the seventy-fifth remembrance. It took him well into January before he went to the gym again.

I asked him if he would like to go anywhere else.

Without hesitation, he said, "The 9/11 Memorial."

John had stayed up for days straight and watched live as the attack unfolded. He was really angry and felt the same hatred he had in his soul after Pearl Harbor until he sat with a Japanese solder at Guadalcanal during the fifty-year remembrance. When he returned home from the fiftieth anniversary of Guadalcanal, much to his surprise, he got a letter from the man postmarked 1992 from his hometown in Japan. It told of how fierce the fighting was and that it was John shooting at him.

Sixty years, later he was watching Pearl Harbor all over again in New York City. He did not settle down or sleep until he saw them raise the American flag over the site.

He went to his garage and created signs that said: "Two days that will live in infamy December 7, 1941 and September 11, 2001."

A short time later, he went on to create a pin that showed the flag being raised over ground zero with a caption: "Out of this twisted steel and smoldering ashes America rises September 11, 2001." John had a hundred made and passed them out to friends.

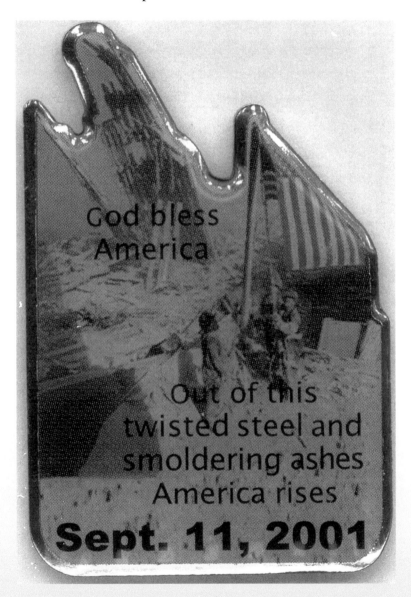

Diane Pirzada, a preservationist and historian, came into the picture by way of her sister, the manager of the Lock and Key restaurant in Englewood Florida.

I went to work collecting information on the 9/11 Memorial to piece together a trip.

When calling the 9/11 Memorial, I told them I was bringing my ninety-four-year-old friend, a Pearl Harbor survivor who would like to pay his respects and see ground zero. They put me on hold, and I was transferred to the business office.

The person on the phone was in shock. "You're bringing who? A real Pearl Harbor survivor? I don't think we've ever had a Pearl Harbor survivor visit."

I said, "That's hard to believe. After all, it's been sixteen years. Someone should have been through."

In the weeks that it took to plan this historic trip, no one could recall seeing a Pearl Harbor survivor at the 9/11 Memorial. John and I could not believe it. I found out that you need a permit for just about anything in New York City. At the 9/11 Memorial or on the plaza, there has to be a well-planned approved permit. The plan was adjusted many times as the knowledge of his trip grew. Finally, after getting frustrated, I proposed my original simple plan.

The staff of the 9/11 Memorial took it from there.

We would fly in on May 14, pay our respects on May 15, and fly out on May 16. That changed when I got a call from Linda Blick, cochair of the Tails of Hope Foundation in New York City. She wanted John to come for Fleet Week at the end of the month. She offered some funding as well as a nice respectful itinerary for his week in New York. There was a GoFundMe page for John's trip to New York City. Two days later, I was contacted by Maverick Johnson, CEO of the Denis V. Cooper Foundation—Wishes for Heroes. He said they were behind us and provided funding for John, Diane, and Emi. I funded myself.

The Denis V. Cooper Foundation asked to meet John for lunch. We showed up at a tavern and met the entire board of directors plus some friends. As we talked, we heard a rumbling outside. The Vietnam Veterans Motorcycle Club had heard John was there with the foundation members, and they stopped by for a very welcomed meet and greet. They presented John with some stars and goodwill, handshakes, and hugs.

Just before lunch, at a corner table, John recounted the morning of December 7, 1941, in a clear voice. Every eye was focused, and every ear was leaning toward him to hear details of that morning that were not in any history book. He recalled a vivid, clear memory of that morning, and you could have heard a pin drop.

I told John I had a surprise to begin the trip.

When I told him I was planning a surprise, he always said, "I hate surprises."

On May 23, 2017, we began our historic trip to New York City with a hero's send-off.

We assembled in a parking lot just down the road from the airport, and we were escorted the last eight miles to the departure concourse in a parade led by Sarasota sheriffs on motorcycles, the Vietnam Veterans Motorcycle Club with American flags, and lighted sheriff vehicles.

At the airport, there were reporters, cameras, a crowd of about seventy, and the CEO and board of trustees from the Denis V. Cooper Foundation.

John got out of the van, and his shorts dropped all the way down to his ankles!

I stepped in front of him and fitted him up, and we rolled forward!

John did three television interviews before heading up the elevator.

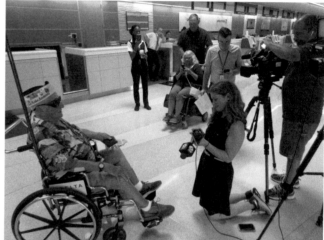

On the second floor, seventy-five people were lined up, and there was an honor guard. We paused to salute, shake hands, and thank everyone attending. There was a thunderous round of applause.

John was humbled at the gate and said, "That was really something." He had no idea it was only the beginning.

We boarded the plane, and John was in row 1, seat 1. Emi sat beside him in first class. It was very important to John that Emi went to New York. He said, "Young people need to remember. If they don't know, they can't remember or share the experiences with other young people."

I sat across the aisle from John and Emi.

The captain made an announcement that John was on board, and we could hear the applause from the front to the back of the plane.

When we landed, John was the last to depart. The handshakes, hugs, and appreciation for him was incredible. We used a lot of hand sanitizer!

When we got off the plane, the first sight we saw was Diane. She had flown in from California for that historic week.

At the hotel, someone noticed that John's luggage—with his medication—was missing.

I called all my contacts in New York, including some of the police chiefs I had been in contact with for John's visit.

The bag was located at the airport, and I hired a cab driver to take the bag directly to me.

We were staying at the Marriott World Trade Center, and they had signs to welcome John. We got him settled in with his luggage and medication, and Diane and I split a bottle of nice red wine in the lobby. Our nerves were frayed, and the wine hit the spot.

The next morning, we were to attend a special gathering sponsored by the Tails of Hope Foundation. Linda Blick and some friends had planned a nice meet and greet.

At about eleven o'clock our first night, the fire alarm went off. It went off again about an hour later, about two hours after that, and then one more time.

John did not sleep, and I did not sleep. Diane was concerned about him.

The Marriott put John up in a large suite with an extra bed. Diane stayed in the bed next to him for most of the night to make certain he was okay.

With plans canceled for that day, we all had a nice breakfast.

John said he would like to go to the 9/11 Memorial's reflecting pools on the plaza to get a feel for the place. We took him in a wheelchair to save his energy.

When we passed a police checkpoint on Liberty Street, the officers came out of the protective shelter and gazed proudly at John.

In the plaza, there were four police officers. A short distance later, there were four more counterterrorism officers who kind of stayed with us. As we walked and looked around, it seemed as though everyone knew who we were, yet we had no idea what to expect. A lot of security followed us as we walked around.

John was greeted warmly by many people. He shook hands, was hugged, and had many picture opportunities.

For dinner, we met Lieutenant Colonel Richard Vargus from the Pentagon.

John wanted to go to some famous New York City steak houses.

We met Lieutenant Colonel Vargus and his wife at Tribeca Palm, and the company and conversation were incredible.

Mary, an assistant for Linda Blick, was in attendance. Diane Pirzada and Emi were there too. The platters of appetizers and steaks were all fit for a survivor!

On May 25, 2017, a footnote to history took place. We all got up early and had breakfast. John had a special bond with Emi. The two of them were talking and smiling. It was more than about the war—it was about youth, remembering, hearing the story firsthand, and passing his legacy to her. Emi is gifted beyond her years, and she is a talented artist.

Before the trip, I had asked Emi to create a special painting that would represent John's historic visit, New York City, the 9/11 Memorial, and Pearl Harbor. Easy, right? We talked about it several times before the trip. The final artwork was going to be an adaptation of all the thoughts we had. The work was finished, placed in a cover, and brought with her.

I wanted it to be special for John.

Nicola Wales-Wong recommended a flower shop that would make a fresh Hawaiian lei that I would have shipped fresh to New York the day before. The florist shop did not like our idea for the lei and said, "It's not pure Hawaiian enough!" They came up with a premium Hawaiian wild double-strung white orchid lei with a blue and red ribbon that would rest over John's heart when he placed it around his neck.

We planned the trip for months. Word must have got around. Someone anonymously sent me a package with no return address and only a Hoboken, New Jersey, postmark. Inside was a forty-eight-star American flag. A small note indicated that the flag had been made in New York and hung in a family hardware store on Ninth Avenue on December 7, 1941. They wanted John to have it to do with as he pleased. Before we into the auditorium, I wrapped the tattered, stained World War II flag around his shoulders. John also brought along a hundred of the pins he had designed in 2001. We had them remade. The only way you could get one of the pins was if he gave it to you.

Three board members from the Denis V. Cooper Foundation flew in from Sarasota to witness and be part of this historic day. John would honor the 9/11 Memorial by wearing his special embroidered "Pearl Harbor 75" shirt along with his dress whites for only the second time after December 7, 2016.

It was pouring rain outside, and there was no letup in the forecast. We planned on placing the lei on the granite reflecting pool. He would turn and salute the other reflecting pool as part of his respects. The plans were being scrambled due to the rain.

A police car escorted John to the 9/11 Memorial. We entered through a side door to the auditorium.

When I wheeled John inside, pipes and drums were playing, an honor guard was saluting, and a lot of members of the military and staff were present.

John turned to me and said, "Is this for me?"

I nodded.

Taps was played, and John was presented with an American flag that had flown over the 9/11 Memorial that morning. John was led to the flag that was raised over the rubble, which had only recently been returned.

John stood up and placed the lei on the case holding the flag. He slowly turned and saluted those lost in the attacks. It was a very touching moment.

Emi unwrapped her painting and placed it next to the lei.

There was a big meet and greet with a lot of pictures and handshakes.

When it stopped raining, the staff placed John's lei on the memorial for the public to view.

John walked over with a tear in his eye and said, "I am glad I got a chance to pay my respects and honor those lost."

Heidi Hayden, chief people officer for the 9/11 Memorial led a tour, and we kept John in his wheelchair to conserve his energy. Robert Reeg, an FDNY firefighter who was pulled from the rubble on 9/11, joined us.

John was mesmerized as he took in the vastness and detail of each exhibit.

Heidi was so kind, and she would often crouch down to talk directly to John at eye level. As we neared the end, Heidi gave John a 9/11 medallion.

At the end of the tour, we were at the main pillar of steel that symbolizes ground zero and the Twin Towers. The names were painted on it in a graffiti style. At the base of the pillar, John took the forty-eight-star flag from around his shoulders and placed it around the neck of 9/11 survivor Robert Reeg. They would forever be brothers, and there was not dry eye in the house.

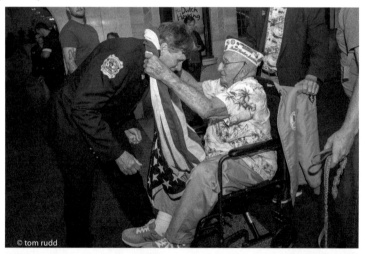

For lunch, we went to a nearby tavern with veterans of the NYPD and FDNY. Some even had service dogs. We shared lots of laughs and emotional moments. It was a really nice lunch.

After lunch, we had a standing invitation to visit Ladder 10 Engine Company, which had been wiped out in the attack. They welcomed John and our entire group with open arms.

Emi tried on one of the firefighters' jackets. It was so heavy! We made our way back so John could take a nap before dinner.

John was invited to the Fleet Week program on the *Intrepid*. We had breakfast in a building near the ship. John was asked to speak, and they asked me to introduce him.

I asked, "How long do I have to think of an introduction?"

They said, "You have about two minutes."

Okay—no pressure!

I introduced John, and he began emotionally talking about Pearl Harbor and Guadalcanal. When he talked of brutal hand-to-hand bayonet fights, he broke down—and so did everyone else. At the end, he said, " I don't know how I lived through it. I don't know why everyone else is gone—and I am still here."

The auditorium erupted in an emotional, tearful standing ovation that seemed to go on for minutes.

In attendance was mayor Bill De Blasio, the CEO and board of directors of the *Intrepid*, the admiral of the Pacific theater, and another Pearl Harbor survivor. The Pearl Harbor survivors sat next to one another in the front row. Diane sat next to John. There were speeches, a large flag was unfurled, with some wreaths were placed in the river.

When it was time to get John on board, there was no handicapped access. He went to the USS Kearsarge.

One of the service captains called four strong service members, and they picked John up in his wheelchair and carried him in! "All aboard!"

John toured the ship in a golf cart. He shook hands and told stories.

I decided to set him up with a martial arts instructor. I asked if he would bust John's chops by telling him he heard that he was a sergeant and got busted to corporal for getting caught gambling. I set John up to bust on this young solder.

I went around the corner to set it up, and then I came back.

John said, "Don't make me get out of this cart, son. I think I have one more good punch in me?"

John was 29–0 with twenty-nine knockouts, and he was scheduled to box the night of the attack. He rattled off the lines, forming a fist with his hand and a huge smile on his face.

The young man smiled and said his lines, and they both had a nice laugh.

John went on to meet and share words with mayor Bill De Blasio.

That night, New Jersey Police Chief Timothy Griffin invited us to dinner at Bobby Van's, another New York steak house.

John was transported via a lighted, unmarked police SUV. He said, "I wonder what all these people pulling over would think if they knew we were only going to dinner!"

The dinner was insanely delicious and decadent. Chief Tim gave John a special plaque and some special-recognition medallions. Staff and patrons in the restaurant came by to shake John's hand or share a smile.

May 28 was to be John's day off to rest up before traveling home.

Heidi Hayden called and asked if John would be interested in showing up for the US Marine Corps marching band performing patriotic numbers on the plaza.

As usual, John said yes and threw himself out there for the public again. John decided to walk to the plaza, which was more than a mile away. He was getting sick of the wheelchair and sitting.

With the chair in tow and the walker in his hands, he began his walk to the plaza.

At every intersection, a police officer stopped traffic for him—as if they knew he was on a mission.

On Liberty Street, he stopped. His shorts were around his ankles again! After pulling them up and cinching his belt, we were underway!

There were thousands of people in the plaza. It was a very different crowd. They seemed to be very aware that John was there, and they knew what he stood for. Some of the people saw John and were really emotional. Some wept. Others just stared. The police protective layer around John was heavy.

John took the time to personally thank many of those around him for providing security. John really wanted to see and hear the Marine Corps band perform. The marines and John were very close, especially the black marines. John fought in hand-to-hand combat on Guadalcanal with them. Many times, he admitted that he owed his life to those marines. As the band marched in precise order, they formed rows on the plaza and began playing the National Anthem.

John had asked me to help him to his feet if they played the National Anthem. As the National Anthem began, he reached to Heidi on one side and Diane on the other and said, "Can you help me to my feet?"

John stood at attention and saluted as the National Anthem was played. Hundreds of cameras snapped pictures of him. At ninety-four, he was standing at attention and saluting the flag. He said, "I won't sit or take a knee for the country I love, the flag, and the National Anthem I fought for."

John went to the survivor tree on the plaza for public handshakes, hugs, and greeting people.

A police car took us to the waterfront to have lunch and visit the Statue of Liberty.

A random New York resident saw us having lunch and picked up the tab for the entire table. He asked to take a picture with John and his young son. He said he would share that picture with his son when he grew up. John boarded the ferry to take in the Statue of Liberty and said, "With all she has stood for, she never stood for more than now"

John said they had the best oyster stew in Grand Central Station. The last time John went there was 1952. Upon arrival, we were all stunned when many NYPD officers and their service dogs were lined up to greet John.

The area was cordoned off from the public, but the public could stop and watch. Hundreds watched, and many took pictures and videos. John went down the line and shook the hands and greeted as many officers as he could.

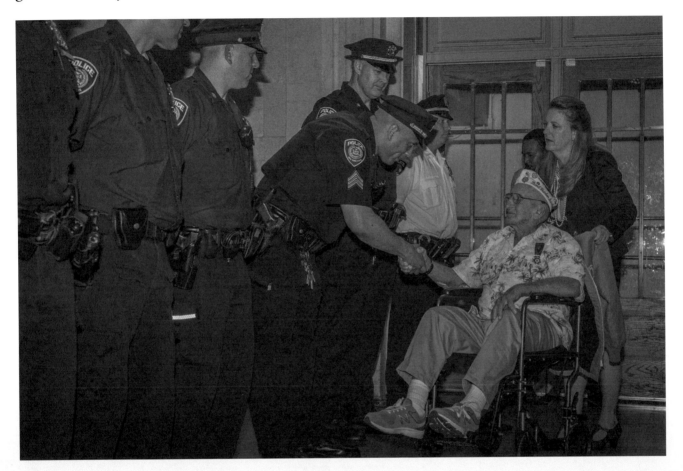

Linda Blick made reservations at the oyster bar for our group of about a dozen—not including service dogs. There was a large table set up for us, but John would have no part of it. He wanted to eat with the people of New York City. He took his walker and walked toward the food service bar, and Diane accompanied him.

There were two chairs open, but they were not together.

John yelled out, "Hey, can everyone move down so this gal can sit next to me?"

The looks on all their faces were typical for New York. When they saw his Pearl Harbor survivor's cover, the whole room changed. Everyone scooted over and made room for them at the counter. The owner and head chef came out, and John ordered the same oyster stew he had in 1952. He said, "Delicious—has not changed a bit!"

The trip home was the same first-class treatment, and passengers were straining to see him or shake his hand. When we got home, he was tired. He was very thankful for the entire trip.

In the weeks and months that followed, John's health was seriously challenged. He had two surgeries and recovered enough to go home again.

It was a tradition for John and I to go to dinner on the national holiday with some friends. On July 4, 2017, while in a rehabilitation facility, he asked me to get his Hawaiian shirt, his Pearl Harbor cover, and some nice pants. The staff at the rehabilitation facility sort of knew his background. To them, John was an old patient who mostly wore pajamas. He cleaned up and put on his clothes and his Pearl Harbor survivor cover.

When John began to walk out with only his walker, the staff stopped in their tracks and stared. Their jaws were open, and their eyes were filled with tears as he exited the building.

A few of us went to dinner at Fins on the Water. The room was abuzz at the sight of this old solder walking in for dinner. The bartenders took care of his drink. The chef came to the table, took his order, personally made his dinner, served it, and picked up the tab.

As John rose to his feet to leave, everyone in the entire restaurant stood and gave him a standing ovation, which caused tears to run down John's face. He turned to me and said, "That was really nice. I did not expect that."

I was humbled.

John passed away on August 11, 2017, at the age of ninety-four years and eight months. Lieutenant Colonel Richard Vargus was the commanding officer for John's funeral, and he was buried with full Military honors in Cleveland Ohio. John Seelie touched the lives of thousands of people. His love for this country came without condition. It was an honor to serve John and know him. He is loved by many, and he is missed. God bless our veterans. God bless the greatest generation. God bless John Seelie. God bless America.

In 2015, I would buy him his beer and something to eat at each Browns game, never indicating that I was the one who did it.

He said, "I don't know who picks up my tab. Do you think I can get away with ordering one of every item on the menu and a full keg of beer?"

We walked into an Italian restaurant, and a very attractive, tall, thin, young waitress walked over to him and said, "Hey, John, are you here to see me—or are you here to get your meatball sandwich?" She gave him a kiss on the cheek.

John said, "I don't always get the meatball sandwich, do I? Pretty sure I come here to see you."

She said, "No. It's pretty much the meatball sandwich."

He said, "Really? Okay. I will have the meatball sandwich."

As we were walking out, he turned to her and said, "Ashley, how tall are you?"

She said, "A little over six foot one. Why?"

John was five foot six, and he turned to her and said "Did you know I am six foot six when I lie down?"

I thought, *John Seelie, put a bar of soap in your mouth.* He knew her well, and they both laughed—and she hugged him and kissed him on the forehead.

Another waitress at the Lock and Key was "working" on him for weeks to take her with him to Hawaii. She said, "I am fun, John. Take me with you."

He had no response at all for a long time. When she went to the kitchen to retrieve something, he leaned over and said, "I bet that would be nice to roll around with."

I must have looked like a deer in headlights.

He said, "Not dead yet!"

John was built like a martini glass. He lost weight during one of his trips, and his shorts and pants were always falling down. Even suspenders did not do the trick because he would forget to wear them. It seemed that when you did not need that to happen, it happened!

ABOUT THE AUTHOR

Mike Cahill is humbled and honored to share these stories of his friend—Pearl Harbor, Guadalcanal, New Georgia Island, and malaria survivor, John Seelie.

About the Book

A Pearl Harbor survivor's love for the United States drives him
from surviving as a front-line combat soldier in some of the toughest
battles in World War II to share his message that war is hell—and
you better think twice about starting one or getting into another
one. This is a seventy-six-year journey to honor and remember those
who served before us, giving us the freedom we have today.

John passes his legacy to our youth to remember Pearl Harbor" Photo taken by Emi Kopke then she created the back cover oil painting.

Printed in the United States
By Bookmasters